BUSINESS VENTURES

DR. ABHISHEK VENKTESHWAR & DR. BHARGAVI D HEMMIGE

ISBN 979-888546120-7

Dedicated to

Aspiring Entrepreneurs!

Contents

Preface

Entrepreneurs are frequently thought of as national assets to be cultivated, motivated and respected to the greatest possible extent.

Business can change the way we live and work. If successful, their innovations may improve our standard of living. In short, in addition to creating wealth from their entrepreneurial ventures, they also create jobs and the conditions for a prosperous society.

Acknowledgements

This book has been a gratifying experience in the journey of our life. We thank God for his blessings in this endeavor.We would like to thank the President-Jain University trust and Chancellor Dr Chenraj Roychand, who has been our mentor and a guiding light. His words of wisdom have inspired us to write this book. We are also grateful to Dr Dinesh Nilkant, Director –JU-CMS for constantly supporting and encouraging us.We also take this opportunity to thank Dr N.Sundarrajan, Pro- Chancellor, Dr Raj Singh, Vice Chancellor, Ms Jayashree and Ms Chaitra Shetty Coordinators- JU-CMS for constantly supporting us in this journey. We would also like to thank our family, friends, colleagues and students for motivating us to write this book.Finally, we are sincerely obliged to all those who have directly or indirectly helped us in the completion of this book.

Prologue

This text book enables the reader to understand the basics of Business Ventures.To sum it up, this book acts as a "one stop shop" for guiding individuals to understand Business Ventures.

ABOUT THE AUTHORS :

Dr. Abhishek Venkteshwar

Dr. Abhishek Venkteshwar is an Assistant Professor, Course Facilitator and Head-Student Council at Center for Management Studies, Jain (Deemed-to-be) University. He is the recipient of three gold medals for Academic excellence in PhD, M.Phil., MBA and B.Sc (Hons). He is UGC-K-SET qualified and certified in University Teaching by Harvard University, Yale University, IIM-Bengaluru and ISB-Hyderabad. Abhishek is a certified awarder in the

'Duke of Edinburgh International Awards'. He was also the Academic Coordinator (Entrepreneurship) at Babson College, USA from 2017-18. He has authored more than 65 papers in several UGC care / Scopus indexed International journals and over 22 books published by Amazon, Notion press, Eureka and Sapna Book House. Abhishek in a span of 8 years has won several awards for teaching and research. He was awarded the most coveted "Best Professor" (Under 30) in RULA International Awards (
2020), Global Leadership Awards (2019) and DR Research Awards (2018). In 2021, he was awarded an honorary doctorate from University of NJ for his contribution to research and teaching (under 30). He has been a part of several panel discussions on the Union Budget on various national television channels.

Dr. Bhargavi D Hemmigeeption

Dr. Bhargavi D Hemmige is currently working as an Associate Professor and Head of the Department - Media Studies at Center for Management Studies, Jain (Deemed-to-be-University). She is also the Chair to Radio Active, the oldest community Radio in Bangalore run by Jain University. Dr Hemmige has over 14 years of experience in teaching and research.

She has also been working with NGOs and stayed associated with government of Karnataka. One of her note-worthy engagements is being the media-co-ordinator to Bengaluru-San Francisco sister city initiative where she closely worked with Mayor of San Francisco, angel investors and government of Karnataka. She has also served as 'Syndicate Member' to the University of Mangalore. She has been inspired by Gandhi and her father-in-law, who has been a freedom fighter. She believes in the soft power of social media to make a difference, at the same time, being concerned about the challenges they bring in. She is a founder member of a society for visually challenged students in Mysuru and has been instrumental in setting up a scribe bank for them. She is passionate towards gender equality, environment and climate change and grassroots media, particularly, community radio. She has completed funded projects on Social Media and Adolescents, Community Radio and been working on a 'Tribal Education Project' and 'Juvenile Home Project'.She believes that Journalism education can be successfully imparted only when the students are exposed to social realities. The focus needs to be on developing critical thinking and learning to make ethical judgements.

Foreword

"This book is an asset to all business houses"

CHAPTER ONE

TOP CEO'S

In This module we will learn :

- *Learn about the role and qualities of CEO'S*
- *Learn about the reasons for attrition of CEO's*
- *Study about one of the world's best CEO in detail.*

INTRODUCTION

A chief executive officer (CEO in American English) or managing director (MD in British English) describes the position of the most senior corporate officer (executive) or administrator in charge of managing a for-profit organization.

WHY CEO 'S KEEP CHANGING?

Attrition is a hot-button issue particularly if its about the CEO of the organisation. What he does in the top jobs sends a clear signal down below.

But if a study done by EMA Partners, an executive search firm, is to be believed than the situation isn't that encouraging. A five-year study done across 100 companies between 2001-06, reveals that a high 66% of the companies has had a change of CEO in the last five years.

There are of course patterns depending on pedigree of the companies and sectors they belonged to. "Not a single company (who were being tracked) sacked its CEO - clearly in India CEOs "resign" never get sacked" says K Sudarshan, managing partner, EMA Partners.Succession planning is the best in companies who are run-managed by professional boards, a reason why they have almost zero churn.

R CEOs in India rarely get sacked - they just resign and move on. Still a substantially high percentage - 24% - change in CEO happen because the CEO is retiring. Change of CEOs due to global transfer is at 17% - perhaps a fair endorsement of the demand of Indian CEOs overseas

Churn due to global transfer

We can see it at HLL, P&G, a large number of banks - FMCG and banking lead in sending Indian CEOs to man other global positions.

Churn in CEOs

There's far more stability at the top in family-owned (understandable because most of the time its the promoter who runs it) and board-run businesses than the headquarter-driven MNCs. Coca Cola has had three CEOs in the last five years.

WORLDS LEADING CEO'S

JEFF BEZOZ

American entrepreneur Jeff Bezos is the founder and chief executive officer of Amazon.com. In 2013, he purchased The Washington Post.

Synopsis

Entrepreneur and e-commerce pioneer Jeff Bezos was born on January 12, 1964, in Albuquerque, New Mexico. Bezos had an early love of computers and studied computer science and electrical engineering at Princeton University. After graduation, he worked on Wall Street, and in 1990 became the youngest senior vice president at the investment firm D.E. Shaw. Four years later, he quit his lucrative job to open Amazon.com, a virtual bookstore that became one of the internet's biggest success stories. In 2013, Bezos made headlines when he purchased*The Washington Post* in a $250 million deal.

Early Life and Career

Jeff Bezos was born on January 12, 1964, in Albuquerque, New Mexico, to a teenage mother, Jacklyn Gise Jorgensen, and his biological father, Ted Jorgensen. Bezos's parents were married less than a year, and when Bezos was four years old his mother married his step-father Mike Bezos, a Cuban immigrant.

As a child, Jeff Bezos showed an early interest in how things work, turning his parents‘ garage into a laboratory and rigging electrical contraptions around his house. As a teenager, his family moved to Miami where he developed a love for computers and excelled in school, becoming the valedictorian of his class. In high school, he also started his first business, the Dream Institute, an educational summer camp for fourth, fifth and sixth graders.

Bezos pursued his interest in computers at Princeton University, where he graduated summa cum laude in 1986 with a degree in computer science and electrical engineering. After graduation, he found work at several firms on Wall Street including Fitel, Bankers Trust, and the investment firm D.E. Shaw where he met his wife Mackenzie and was named the youngest vice president in 1990. While his career in finance was extremely lucrative, Bezos chose to make a risky move into the nascent world of e-commerce. He quit his job in 1994, moved to Seattle and targeted the untapped potential of the internet market by opening an online bookstore.

Pioneering E-Commerce

Bezos then moved Amazon into the tablet marketplace with the unveiling of the Kindle Fire in 2011. The following September, he announced the new Kindle Fire HD, the company's next generation tablet designed to give Apple's iPad a run for its money. "We haven't built the best tablet at a certain price. We have built the best tablet at any price," Bezos said, according to ABC News.

Buying 'The Washington Post'

Bezos made headlines worldwide on August 5, 2013, when he purchased *The Washington Post* and other publications affiliated with The Washington Post Co., which owns the paper and other entities, for $250 million cash. The deal marks the end of the four-generation reign over The Post Co. by the Graham family, including Donald E. Graham, the company's chairman and chief executive, and his niece, *Post*publisher Katharine Weymouth.

"*The Post* could have survived under the company's ownership and been profitable for the foreseeable future," Graham stated, in an effort to explain the transaction. "But we wanted to do more than survive. I'm not saying this guarantees success, but it gives us a much greater chance of success."

In a statement to *Post* employees on August 5, Bezos wrote: "The values of *The Post* do not need changing. ...There will, of course, be change at *The Post*over the coming years. That's essential and would have happened with or without new ownership. The internet is transforming almost every element of the news business: shortening news cycles, eroding long-reliable revenue sources, and enabling new kinds of competition, some of which bear little or no news-gathering costs. There is no map, and charting a path ahead will not be easy. We will need to invent, which means we will need to experiment. Our touchstone will be readers, understanding what they care about—government, local leaders, restaurant openings, scout troops, businesses, charities, governors, sports—and working backwards from there. I'm excited and optimistic about the opportunity for invention."

Recent Projects

In early December 2013, Bezos made headlines when he revealed a new, experimental initiative by Amazon, called "Amazon Prime Air," using drones—remote-controlled machines that can perform an array of human tasks—to provide delivery services to customers. According to Bezos, these drones are able to carry items weighing up to 5 pounds, and are capable of traveling within a 10-mile distance of the company's distribution center. He also stated that Prime Air could become a reality within as little as four or five years.

MARK ZUCKERBERG

Mark Zuckerberg is co-founder and CEO of the social-networking website Facebook, as well as one of the world's youngest billionaires.

Synopsis

Born on May 14, 1984, in White Plains, New York, Mark Zuckerberg co-founded the social-networking website Facebook out of his college dorm room. He left Harvard after his sophomore year to concentrate on the site, the user base of which has grown to more than 250 million people, making Zuckerberg a billionaire. The birth of Facebook was recently portrayed in the film *The Social Network*.

Early Life

Mark Elliot Zuckerberg was born on May 14, 1984, in White Plains, New York, into a comfortable, well-educated family, and raised in the nearby village of Dobbs Ferry. His father, Edward Zuckerberg, ran a dental practice attached to the family's home. His mother, Karen, worked as a psychiatrist before the birth of the couple's four children—Mark, Randi, Donna and Arielle.

Zuckerberg developed an interest in computers at an early age; when he was about 12, he used Atari BASIC to create a messaging program he named "Zucknet." His father used the program in his dental office, so that the receptionist could inform him of a new patient without yelling across the room. The family also used Zucknet to communicate within the house. Together with his friends, he also created computer games just for fun. "I had a bunch of friends who were artists," he said. "They'd come over, draw stuff, and I'd build a game out of it."

To keep up with Mark's burgeoning interest in computers, his parents hired private computer tutor David Newman to come to the house once a week and work with

Mark. Newman later told reporters that it was hard to stay ahead of the prodigy, who began taking graduate courses at nearby Mercy College around this same time.

Zuckerberg later studied at Phillips Exeter Academy, an exclusive preparatory school in New Hampshire. There he showed talent in fencing, becoming the captain of the school's team. He also excelled in literature, earning a diploma in classics. Yet Zuckerberg remained fascinated by computers, and continued to work on developing new programs. While still in high school, he created an early version of the music software Pandora, which he called Synapse. Several companies—including AOL and Microsoft—expressed an interest in buying the software, and hiring the teenager before graduation. He declined the offers.

Time at Harvard

After graduating from Exeter in 2002, Zuckerberg enrolled at Harvard University. By his sophomore year at the ivy league institution, he had developed a reputation as the go-to software developer on campus. It was at that time that he built a program called CourseMatch, which helped students choose their classes based on the course selections of other users. He also invented Facemash, which compared the pictures of two students on campus and allowed users to vote on which one was more attractive. The program became wildly popular, but was later shut down by the school administration after it was deemed inappropriate.

Based on the buzz of his previous projects, three of his fellow students—Divya Narendra, and twins Cameron and Tyler Winklevoss—sought him out to work on an idea for a social networking site they called Harvard Connection.

This site was designed to use information from Harvard's student networks in order to create a dating site for the Harvard elite. Zuckerberg agreed to help with the project, but soon dropped out to work on his own social networking site with friends Dustin Moskovitz, Chris Hughes and Eduardo Saverin.

Zuckerberg and his friends created a site that allowed users to create their own profiles, upload photos, and communicate with other users. The group ran the site—first called The Facebook—out of a dorm room at Harvard until June 2004. After his sophomore year, Zuckerberg dropped out of college to devote himself to Facebook full time, moving the company to Palo Alto, California. By the end of 2004, Facebook had 1 million users.

The Rise of Facebook

Although an initial settlement of $65 million was reached between the two parties, the legal dispute over the matter continued well into 2011, after Narendra and the Winklevosses claimed they were misled in regards to the value of their stock.

Zuckerberg faced yet another personal challenge when the 2009 book *The Accidental Billionaires*, by writer Ben Mezrich, hit stores. Mezrich was heavily criticized for his re-telling of Zuckerberg's story, which used invented scenes, re-imagined dialogue and fictional characters. Regardless of how true-to-life the story was, Mezrich managed to sell the rights of the tale to screenwriter Aaron Sorkin, and the critically acclaimed film *The Social Network* received eight Academy Award nominations.Zuckerberg objected strongly to the film's narrative, and later told a reporter at *The New Yorker* that many of the details in the film were inaccurate. For example, Zuckerberg has been dating longtime girlfriend Priscilla Chan, a Chinese-American medical student he met at Harvard, since 2003. He also said he never had interest in joining any of the final clubs. "It's interesting what stuff they focused on getting right; like, every single shirt and fleece that I had in that movie is actually a shirt or fleece that I own," Zuckerberg told a reporter at a start-up conference in 2010. "So there's all this stuff that they got wrong and a bunch of random details that they got right."

Yet Zuckerberg and Facebook continued to succeed, in spite of the criticism. *Time* magazine named him Person of the Year in 2010, and *Vanity Fair* placed him at the top of their New Establishment list. *Forbes* also ranked Zuckerberg at No. 35—beating out Apple CEO Steve Jobs—on its "400" list, estimating his net worth to be $6.9 billion.

Philanthropic Causes

Since amassing his sizeable fortune, Zuckerberg has used his millions to fund a variety of philanthropic causes. The most notable examples came in 2010. In September of that year, he donated $100 million to save the failing Newark Public Schools system in New Jersey. Then, in December 2010, Zuckerberg signed the "Giving Pledge", promising to donate at least 50 percent of his wealth to charity over the course of his lifetime. Other Giving Pledge members include Bill Gates, Warren Buffett and George Lucas. After his donation, Zuckerberg called on other young, wealthy entrepreneurs to follow suit. "With a generation of younger folks who have thrived on the success of their companies, there is a big opportunity for many of us to give back earlier in our lifetime and see the impact of our philanthropic efforts," he said.

Going Public

Zuckerberg made two major life changes in May 2012. Facebook had its initial public offering, which raised $16 billion, making it the biggest internet IPO in history. How Zuckerberg's company will handle this influx of cash remains to be seen. But Zuckerberg may be looking at more acquisitions. He personally negotiated the company deal to buy Instragram the previous month.

After the initial success of the IPO, the Facebook stock price dropped somewhat in the early days of trading. But Zuckerberg is expected to weather any ups and downs in his company's market performance. He holds more than a quarter of its stock and retains 57 percent control of the voting shares.

On May 19, 2012—a day after the IPO—Zuckerberg wed his longtime girlfriend, Priscilla Chan. About 100 people gathered at the couple's Palo Alto, California home. The guests thought they were there to celebrate Chan's graduation from medical school, but instead they witnessed Zuckerberg and Chan exchange vows.

In May 2013, Facebook made the *Fortune* 500 list for the first time—making Zuckerberg, at the age of 28, the youngest CEO on the list.

INDRA NOOYI

The lady with a fizz, Indra Krishnamurthy Nooyi is the chairman and CEO of PepsiCo, the world's fourth-largest food and Beverage Company. An Indian-born American executive, Nooyi was ranked No.4 on Forbes magazine's annual survey of the 100 most powerful women in the world. Prior to becoming CEO she was the President, Chief Financial Officer and a member of the Board of Directors of PepsiCo Inc.Belonging to a South Indian family, Nooyi was born on October 28, 1955 in Tamil Nadu, India. Her father worked at the State Bank of Hyderabad and her grandfather was a district judge. She completed her schooling from Holy Angels AIHSS, Chennai and received a Bachelor's degree in Physics, Chemistry and Maths from Madras Christian College in 1974. On completion of her graduation she went to Indian Institute of Management (IIM) Calcutta for doing Masters in Finance and Marketing. According to the faculty members Nooyi has been a very mediocre student.

Early Life

After completion of her MBA she joined ABB and then Johnson and Johnson (J&J) in Mumbai as a product manager. One of her achievement with J&J is her close association with launch of the sanitary napkin, Stayfree. Not satisfied with the way her career was going she persuaded her parents to let her study at Yale Management School in US and earned a Master's degree in Public and Private Management in 1978.

While studying at Yale she worked as a receptionist to buy a western suit for her first job interview. Being uncomfortable with the outfit she was rejected. For her next interview her professor advised her to stick to what she was comfortable with. She wore a sari and got the job and this philosophy of 'be yourself' she followed for the rest of her career.

Before landing in Pepsi, world's second largest soft-drink company Nooyi worked with Boston Consulting Group and Motorola. Nooyi coaxed the CEO Roger Enrico of the Pepsi to follow-up the company's restaurant division, including brands such KFC, Pizza Hut and Taco Bell, as the chief strategy officer.

Entry into the big league

Transformation

She steered PepsiCo with revenues of more than USD 60 billion and over 285,000 employees. She equally emphasized in the Mergers and Acquisition which was bolstered by the acquisition of the Tropicana and Quaker fruit juice brands. With her superb knack of facts and figures she predicted the slowdown in the popularity of aerated soft drinks in the markets worldwide. She meticulously planned for the foray of Pepsi into the sport drinks market in association with Gatorade. Her quick decision making ability and clinging to the work until it's accomplished continues to grow PepsiCo, the USD 39 billion food and beverage giant.

Focusing on innovation instead of acquisition, the company has been debuting new product lines, targeted marketing and repackaging efforts since 2009. The group also launched a "Refresh Everything" campaign, featuring Pepsi Natural, made with all-natural ingredients, and Pepsi and Mountain Dew Throwback, inspired by designs of the 1960s and '70s.

Speaking of her achievements, Nooyi is the 12th highest paid corporate woman in the US, with an annual pay package of over USD 12.7 million, according to Forbes magazine. She shares the world's most 100 most powerful women list with the likes of Condoleeza Rice, Sonia Gandhi, Oprah Winfrey and Hilary Clinton. She was awarded the Padma Bhushan in 2007. Nooyi has been named the 'Most Powerful Business Woman in the world' in 2006 and 2007 by Fortune magazine. Presently, there are only 10 Fortune 500 companies that are run by women. Nooyi is the 11th to break into the top echelons of power. The Cola giant chairperson serves as an Honorary Co-Chair for the World Justice Project.

CHAPTER TWO

LEADERSHIP

DEFINING LEADERSHIP

"Leadership: the art of getting someone else to do something you want to be done because he wants to do it." **— Dwight D. Eisenhower**

"Leadership is the lifting of man's vision to higher sights, the raising man's performance to a higher standard, the building of man's personality beyond its normal limitation." — **Peter F Drucker.**

"Leadership is the ability to secure desirable actions from a group of followers voluntarily without the use of coercion." — **Alford and Beatty.**

"Leadership is the ability to persuade others to seek defined objectives enthusiastically" — **Keith Davis**

"Leadership is the ability to influence people to strive willingly for mutual objectives"

— G R Terry

Hence, from the above definitions, we can infer that Leadership is the knack of getting the efforts of the followers together for the achievement of the goals and objectives of both the individuals and the organization.

DIFFERENTIATING A LEADER FROM A MANAGER

Leadership is the ability to influence a group/team towards the achievement of goals and objectives. Management is the use of established formal authority in a designated hierarchy to obtain compliance from the employees. The following are some of the differences between leaders and managers:

- **Innovators v/s Administrators:** Leader is a person who is full of innovative ideas and who is open to experimentation and developing new things. Leaders are far-sighted and look at the latest trends in the environment to be ahead than the competitors. Managers are people who are executing the tasks as per what is already established in the company and are responsible for all the activities throughout the organizational structure. They control the functioning of the organization.
- **Trust & results v/s control & authority:** A leader inspires others through his vision, attitude, and action. Hence, the followers develop trust and confidence in their leader. A leader builds the right rapport with the team/group of employees and drives them to achieve excellence. In contrast, managers are responsible for maintaining rules and regulations. Hence they are authoritative and control the employees' activities. Their focus is on improving the assets of the organization through established policies and programs.
- **What and why questions v/s how and when questions:** If the employees do not execute the tasks assigned to them as per the expectation, leaders ask questions in

what and why as they are concerned about the development of the individuals along with the organization. However, managers ask questions in how and when in order to understand the reasons for the failure in doing the work, as managers have to keep a check on the activities to track the progress with the set objectives.

- **Solutions v/s strategies:** A leader will look at the hurdles and challenges from a different angle and devise mechanisms to bring out the best possible out of the employees by motivating and encouraging them. Managers create strategies for the execution of the objectives of the company and will empower people by listening to their views and suggestions.
- **Followers v/s Subordinates:** Managers consider the employees working under them as subordinates. This brings in a feeling of being superior to the employees and will try and execute their positional power in the wrong way. However, Leaders consider the employees as followers and believe that the employees have their own individualistic way of executing things along with the inspiration of the leader.

CHARACTERISTICS OF LEADERSHIP

- Leadership refers to the ability of one individual to influence others. Leadership implies the existence of followers.
- Leadership transforms people's potential into reality.
- Leadership is not merely directing people for the achievement of goals of the organization. It has a vision

of empowering the level of human conduct and ethical aspiration of both the leader and the followers.

- The leaders elevate, inspire, and evangelize their followers to higher things in life.
- Leadership involves the change of behavior and attitude of the followers in a positive manner in order to achieve a shared goal.
- It is a group phenomenon having an interaction between two or more people.

IMPORTANCE OF LEADERSHIP IN ORGANISATIONS

According to Peter F Drucker, good leadership is a must for the success of a business but it is the scarcest resource available in any enterprise. Organizations grow when the employees perform their best. Higher the motivation for the employees, usually better is their performance. A good leader directs his followers in a way that they feel encouraged to work in the organization.

In Harvard Business Review, speaking about the leadership lessons from India (March 2010 issue), it was found that Indian leaders scored high on "transformational" or charismatic leadership designed to encourage employees to care about the goals of the leader and the organization. The scores were compared to the U.S CEOs, and it was found that they were "transactional leaders" – motivating employees only based on the interest of the business. However, both the countries' leaders attributed the success of their companies to employees' positive attitude, persistence and sense of reciprocity.

(*Source:* https://hbr.org/2010/03/leadership-lessons-from-india)

Effective leaders sustain and improve the employee morale which increases the productivity and stability in the organization. The social skill of leadership influences the employees' potential towards the growth of an organization. Employees and shareholders of the massive corporate failures at the beginning of this century know to their cost that leadership matters. Those who lost their jobs, pensions, or saw billions wiped off of the value of the organizations they had a stake in, will be aware that the plight of these organizations was not caused by externalities such as world recession or competitor activity. These failures were the direct result of poor leadership. And traits such as narcissism, greed, and criminality have all been recruited to help explain the behavior of the business leaders involved.

CASE IN POINT

Organizations facing leadership 'capability gap' - HR magazine UK, 29th Apr 2015

Organizations are facing a leadership "capability gap" and cite leadership as one of their biggest challenges, according to a research by Deloitte. The firm's UK Human Capital Trends 2015 report found 86% of UK organizations say leadership is one of their biggest challenges. Only 8% ranked their leadership pipeline as 'excellent'. The research also highlighted a capability gap. The difference between the importance of leadership and how ready organizations feel they are to succeed in this area has risen to 35, the widest gap of any HR issue in the report.

It also found businesses are falling short in developing millennial leaders, as only 6% of companies said they have "excellent" programs in place for younger staff. Deloitte

UK's head of human capital practice, Anne-Marie Malley warned that firms need to "urgently address" this issue.

"By 2025, Millennials will represent three-quarters of the workforce," she said. "With four million Baby Boomers retiring each year, Millennials will become ever more important to organizations, and shape the world of work in the future. And yet our research shows a clear lack of commitment to this vital group's development." Learning and development are another key concern for UK businesses, with organizations ranking it the fourth most pressing challenge, up from 11th in 2014.

While 80% of UK businesses said workforce capability was an important challenge, only 4% said they were "very ready" to address it. The research suggests organizations are also missing out on the benefits of using technology to support learning, with only 8% saying they are excellent at providing mobile learning. The HR function, in particular, is also missing out on learning opportunities, with no respondents feeling their organization provides "excellent" development for HR.

Only one in 10 (10%) rated the performance of their HR as excellent and 66% said the functions are ill-equipped to manage the fast pace of change in their businesses. Malley said HR is now expected to be "bold, agile, business-integrated, data-driven and deeply skilled in attracting, retaining and developing talent, to align to the overall goals of the organization." She added: "Companies are seeing an increasing demand for leadership at all levels, especially among Millennials. However, improvements are not coming through fast enough. It is clear that something needs to change in order for UK businesses to effectively navigate the new world of work."

Source: http://www.hrmagazine.co.uk/hro/news/1151093/organisations-facing-leadership capability-gap

ARE LEADERS BORN OR MADE?

Human beings enter this world with many abilities and talents. Some of the leaders are born with traits and then nurtured to become good leaders. However, most of them grow as a leader in the organization due to various experiences. Thus leaders are both born and made. If one has willpower and desire, they can become effective leaders. Leaders develop through a lifelong process of self-study, training, education and experience. One of the unique qualities of great leaders is that they try to develop the leadership skills in their followers so as to create more leaders. Leadership is an art rather than a science. It involves a set of innate traits which are refined and improved over time.

LEADERSHIP THEORIES

Leadership theories have been an essential element in identifying and developing leaders in today's workforce.

Leadership theories evolved over a period of time. Bernard Bass's (1989 & 1990) theory of leadership states that there are three basic ways to explain how people become leaders.

These theories are:

- Some personality traits may lead people naturally into leadership roles - Trait Theory.
- People can choose to become leaders. People can learn leadership skills - Transformational Leadership Theory.

It is the most widely accepted theory today.

- A crisis or important event may cause a person to rise to the occasion, which brings out extraordinary leadership qualities in an ordinary person- Great Events Theory.

Major classification of leadership theories are as follows:
1. Trait Theory (the 1940s)
2. Behavioral Theory (the 1950s)
3. Contingency Theory(the 1960s)

1. TRAIT THEORY

Trait Theory proposes that there are traits which set apart a leader from a nonleader. It assumes that leaders are born and not made. It explains that successful leaders have the right combination of traits which makes their leadership effective in an organization. The interests, personality, abilities of successful leaders are different from less effective leaders. Gordon Allport, an American psychologist identified some specific traits connected to personality , which could be the bottom line of trait theory. Trait theory of leadership tries to analyze mental, physical and social characteristics to correlate the traits which contribute to a particular leadership style. A study conducted by Judge, Bono, Iles and Gerhardt(2002), found that the Big Five personality dimensions (i.e., agreeableness, conscientiousness, extraversion, neuroticism, and openness) were significant predictors of both leadership emergence and leader effectiveness. There exist some core traits which are associated with successful leadership. They are:

- Drive

- Desire to lead
- Honesty and integrity
- Self-confidence
- Intelligence
- Job-relevant knowledge
- Extraversion

Ex: Indira Nooyi, CEO and board chairman of PepsiCo is described as fun-loving, sociable, agreeable, emotionally intelligent and open to experiences. Her personality traits have added to the job performance and career success.

LEADERSHIP CAN BE AN INHERITED TRAIT!!! – Jan 15, 2013

The study, published in *Leadership Quarterly*, is the first to identify a specific DNA sequence associated with the tendency for individuals to occupy a leadership position. Using a large twin sample OF 4000 individuals, the international research team, which included academics from Harvard, NYU, and the University of California, estimate that a quarter of the observed variation in leadership behavior between individuals can be explained by genes passed down from their parents. "We have identified a genotype, called ` 4950, which appears to be associated with the passing of leadership ability down through generations," said lead author Dr Jan-Emmanuel De Neve (UCL School of Public Policy). "The conventional wisdom – that leadership is a skill – remains largely true, but we show it is also, in part, a genetic trait."

Source:http://phys.org/news/2013-01-born-leadership-inherited-trait.html

Some other researchers attribute the following traits for successful leadership – High intellectual ability, Initiative, Imagination, Emotional stability, Desire to accept responsibility, Flexibility, Honesty, Sincerity, Courage, Reliability, Integrity, Persuasive power, Approachability, Forgiveness etc.,

Strengths/Advantages of Trait Theory

- It is clear and easy to understand.
- Through Trait Theory, originations could develop leadership qualities in various employees by nurturing them with the traits that create successful leaders.
- Many research studies have validated the principles of this theory.
- It acts as a standard against which the leadership qualities of an individual can be assessed.

Limitations of the Trait Theory

- It is subjective in judgment while assigning which of the traits make a "good" and a "successful" leader.
- It focuses only on the traits of the individuals and doesn't consider the environment or the situation.
- It doesn't substantially account for personality changes.
- The model also considers physical traits such as height and weight etc. to effective leadership. These factors are situational and would vary between individuals. Ex: In a Military leadership position, a certain height and weight might be necessary. However, business leaders need not have such requirements.

Implications of Trait Theory

Leaders have a focused vision and are powerful in their thoughts. The core traits of the Trait Theory could be modeled and imparted to the employees so that they could build leadership qualities through training and development. While selecting candidates, leadership abilities can be assessed by using the Trait Theory as a yardstick. It would add value to the selection process as the employer could plan to hire candidates and place them in the departments where leadership qualities are necessary.

10 Traits of Great Business Leaders – Forbes – 09/05/2014

Whether you're a freelancer, small-business owner, or full-timer, to climb the ladder, you must know how to lead the pack. Are you destined to be the big boss or be bossed around? To find out, take a look at these 10 characteristics shared by great business leaders:

1. Persistence, Persistence, Persistence

In the 1890s, Henry Ford came up with the Ford Quadricycle, a vehicle made up of a frame mounted on four large bicycle wheels with an ethanol-powered engine. Needless to say, it wasn't a success. Ford later founded the Ford Motor Company, invented the Model T, and became one of the wealthiest men in the world. Do you try, fail, and pick yourself back up again?

2. Thick skin. Rhino-thick.

Walt Disney's editor at the Kansas City Star told him that he had no good ideas and lacked imagination. He could have taken the harsh words to heart and given up the creativity ghost. Instead he went on to become the most successful animator of all time, winning 22 Academy Awards, creating characters like Mickey Mouse, and opening his own theme park. Today, Walt Disney is one of the world's most ubiquitous household name brands, synonymous with creativity.

3. An Eye for Talent

It takes a village to make amazing things happen. That's why great leaders surround themselves with other great minds. Steve Jobs was always on the hunt for talent in unique ways, like accepting invitations to lecture at universities so he could scout potential employees. Jobs personally interviewed over 5,000 applicants during his lifetime, managing all the hiring for his team.

4. Can't Get No Satisfaction

What do Google, Yahoo, and Facebook have in common? All are billion dollar companies that started in dorm rooms. Great business leaders are never satisfied and continually strive to take their business to the next level. As Ingvar Kamprad, the founder of IKEA, said, "The most dangerous poison is the feeling of achievement. The antidote is to every evening think what can be done better tomorrow."

5. Fearlessness

When Richard Branson was younger, his aunt bet him that he couldn't learn to swim during their family vacation. After failing to master the skill during the trip, on the drive home, he asked his father to pull over the car. He jumped into a river, swam, and won the bet. Today, Branson, the founder of the Virgin Group, which is made up of over 400 companies, believes in a philosophy of taking risks and stepping out of your comfort zone. "You don't learn to walk by following rules," Branson said. "You learn by doing, and by falling over."

6. Owning Your Mistakes

After Amazon deleted copies of unauthorized versions of Animal Farm and 1984 from users' Kindles, there was an immediate negative backlash. Not only did Amazon cop to the mistake in an official press statement, CEO Jeff Bezos personally apologized, admitting that the company's solution to the problem was "stupid, thoughtless, and painfully out of line with our principles." He also offered, "deep apologies to our customers."

7. Toughness

If you want to lead in the business world, you're going to have to stand up for yourself. "When somebody challenges you, fight back. Be brutal, be tough," advised Donald Trump. Michael Bloomberg agreed, saying at a commencement ceremony that, "In the business world, it's dog-eat-dog," and, "you occasionally have to throw some elbows."

8. Winning Friends and Influencing People

But don't take the tough act too far. People work better for managers they like. John D. Rockefeller said, "The ability to deal with people is as purchasable as a commodity as sugar or coffee and I will pay more for that ability than for any other thing under the sun." Mark Cuban put things a little more simply: "People hate dealing with people who are jerks. It's always easier to be nice than to be a jerk. Don't be a jerk."

9. Singular Vision

It all starts with an idea. Howard Schultz envisioned a single brand with coffeehouses across the globe. He turned that dream into a reality and founded Starbucks. "I think if you're an entrepreneur, you've got to dream big, and then dream bigger," he said. "It's seeing what other people don't see and pursuing that vision."

10. Powerfully Passionate

Above all, a true leader is passionate about whatever venture he or she is undertaking. As Jobs said, "You have to be burning with an idea, or a problem, or a wrong that you want to right. If you're not passionate enough from the start, you'll never stick it out." Oprah Winfrey also had some powerful words on the subject. "Passion is energy," she said. "Feel the power that comes from doing whatever excites you."

Source: http:// www.forbes.com /sites/ michakaufman/ 2014/09/05/10-traits- of-great-business-leaders/2

2. BEHAVIORAL THEORY

Behavioral theories brought in a new perspective to the context of leadership theory. As opposed to the trait theory , which fixes mental , physical and social traits as determinants for leadership, behavioral theory focuses on the behavior of leaders . Behavioral Theory proposes that certain specific behaviors differentiate leaders from non-leaders. It emphasizes the actual behavior of the individuals rather than trait and characteristics. Effective role behavior is the base for strong and successful leadership. It focuses on observable actions and reactions of the leaders as well as the followers in any situation. This theory supports that leaders can be made. The leader's behavior predicts the leadership influence which best determines the leadership success. Some of the functional behavior of successful leaders are determining goals, motivating employees, effective communication, building team spirit etc.,

It propagates that favorable behavior from the leader motivates the followers who execute their work with greater satisfaction and recognize him as their leader.

Researchers studying this theory evaluated what successful leaders did, developed a catalog of actions and identified patterns that indicated different leadership styles. It is a big leap from Trait Theory as it propagates that leadership capability can be learned and need not be always inherent.

There are two important behavioral studies:

a. Ohio State University: In 1940's they conducted a study that certain traits don't yield any results. They developed a list of 150 statements from 1800 responses. It measured 9 different behavioral leadership dimensions. It is now well-known as LBDQ – Leaders Behavior Description Questionnaire. It was given to various groups of individuals to college students, their administrators, military personnel and few private companies. Common leadership behaviors were identified. After analyzing and interpreting the results, it was concluded that there are two types of leaders – Task-oriented leaders & People-oriented leaders.

- Task-oriented leaders: They are transactional in nature. Their efforts are focused on the organizational structure, policies, procedures etc. They are concerned about the employee morale and motivation; however, it is not their main concern. Initiation, Organization, Clarification, Information gathering etc. are some of the fields of interest for task oriented leaders and they favor behaviors related to these aspects.

Task oriented leader – Carol Bartz

When Yahoo's growth and revenues slowed for several years, the company hired Carol Bartz as its new chief executive. Known as a task oriented leader, Bartz previously led a successful turnaround at software maker

Autodesk where, under her leadership, the company's revenues grew from $300 million to more than $1.5 billion. But after two and a half years at Yahoo, Bartz was fired as CEO for failing to revive the company's revenues and stock price. According to Fiedler's contingency model, Bartz's task oriented style was not effective in improving Yahoo's performance. Observers noted that Bartz failed to provide the visionary leadership and focused strategic direction and execution needed to position the company for growth.

Source: Organizational Behavior 15th Edition - By *Stephen P. Robbins, Timothy A. Judge*

- People-oriented leaders: They are transformational in nature. Their focus is on fulfilling the innate needs of the employees. They motivate the employees and give importance to the human relation. However, they even focus on tasks and results. But they achieve it through the co-operation of other employees. Encouragement, Observation, Listening, Mentoring, Coaching etc. are some of the behaviors exhibited by people oriented leaders.

b. University of Michigan: In 1950's, Dr. Renis Likert leads a study at the University of Michigan and identified three characteristics of effective and efficient leadership. Two of them were already observed in the Ohio State University. The third characteristic was found to be more significant than task and relationship oriented leadership. It was "Participative Leadership." In such style of leadership, the leader involves all the members of the team to set objectives and procedures to achieve such objectives. It involves active participation from all the members who can demonstrate their creativity.

In the initial studies on Behavioral theory, Kurt Lewin and his co-researchers at University of Iowa identified three leadership styles:

1. **Autocratic Style:** It is a classical style of leadership where manager retains the power and has the decision-making authority.

2. **Democratic Style:** It is a participative style of leadership where employees are coached by the leader and share decision-making and problem-solving responsibilities.

3. **Laissez Faire:** It is the hands-off approach of leadership where the responsibilities are shared by all. They receive very little guidance from the leaders and the group members are expected to execute activities on their own.

CASE IN POINT

RECENT SURVEY REVEALS FOUR OF THE TOP LEADERSHIP BEHAVIORS – Forbes – 17/03/2015

There's a leadership gap that exists in the industry today. In government, education, business and non-profit sectors, leadership have become an exception rather than the rule due mainly to the "me" centric approach that governs self-interest. If leadership is about authentic self-expression that inspires others to act or think in a certain way, then when was the last time you were led by someone?

A recent McKinsey & Company study looked at just this. Specifically, researchers asked 189,000 people in 81 different companies across the globe what types of leadership behaviors they esteemed (and therefore sought to apply within their organization), and which ones they wanted to avoid like the uninvited guest at your last party.

Here are the top leadership behaviors people espouse:

Leaders are doers. For lack of a better word that could potentially ban me from the Forbes contributor sphere forever, leaders get "stuff" done. They understand the big picture and clearly assign roles, responsibilities, and expectations that will lead the company in the right direction. Additionally, they work with a laser-like focus on the priorities that drive value, such as building the company and managing relationships. Moreover, they focus on the business rather than on your business.

They seek diversity of thought. Leaders—the smart ones—know that if they want to improve themselves and their company that the only way to do so is to surround themselves with people smarter and more experienced than themselves. Nobody learns from dummies. Sorry, but it's true. Actually, I take that back. We can all learn what not to do. However, in the leadership realm, listening to diverse perspectives only serves you (if you're the leader) to make better, more informed decisions. Can't find anybody? Woe is me. Effective leaders also have a mentor or coach who questions their thought processes and forces them to grow—as people, and as leaders.

Leaders show support. Leaders have a thankless job sometimes. Not only are they expected to know their role as leaders, but also the roles of their people. They must be emotional, socially, and self-aware enough to know when to promote, grow, and challenge their people. Furthermore, they oftentimes have to resolve conflict and make difficult decisions that support the best interest of the company rather than themselves.

They solve problems. Leadership entails making difficult decisions, but that only comes after you have solved the problem. The most effective leaders solve problems by sharing information up, down, and across the corporate chain (of command) because doing so feeds back into the diversity of thought above.

Although the McKinsey survey only highlighted four leadership behaviors, I would add a fifth item to the list and that is problem recognition. Before any solving can take place, you must first isolate the problem, which is not a natural skill. Doing so necessitates a contextual awareness of the environment–and oftentimes, training–since so many internal and external factors come into play. Different stakeholder interests, politics and relationships, minimal resources, and time all have the potential to contribute to the problem, and knowing how to recognize those factors will either help the problem rise to the surface, or keep it hidden below.

Everybody has their own interpretation of the "ideal" leadership behaviors they espouse. What are the leadership gaps that you see in your organization? More so, how can they be filled?

Source: http://www.forbes.com/sites/jeffboss/2015/03/17/recent-survey-reveals-4-of-the-top-leadership-behaviors/

Advantages of Behavioral Theory of Leadership:

- It propagates the theory that "Leaders can be made."
- It helps managers understand and evaluate how their behaviors can affect their rapport with the employees and how it could be used to enhance the subordinate's productivity.
- Participative decision-making style promotes team development and motivates employees to work towards

organizational objectives.

- Criticism / Arguments against - Behavioral Theory of Leadership:
- It doesn't consider the environment in which the behaviors are demonstrated.
- It is unrealistic to expect that a set of beliefs can work under all circumstances
- Since the personality of individuals differs from one another the set of behaviors which makes a successful leader might not be practiced by everyone.

Implications of Behavioral Theory:

The best leaders are those who are adaptable and flex their behavioral style as per the surroundings. They choose the right style suitable to the environment. Leadership can be learned through observation and teaching certain patterns of behavior.

MANAGERIAL GRID THEORY- ONE OF THE BEHAVIOURAL LEADERSHIP THEORIES.

Managerial Grid was developed by Robert Blake and Jane Mouton in 1964. The leaders can have 81 leadership styles. But the managerial grid identifies five leadership styles based on two dimensions:

- Concern for people: It refers to the degree to which the leader considers the employees' needs while making any decisions relating to work. It is the Y axis which runs vertically from bottom to top of the managerial grid.

- Concern for production: It refers to the degree to which leader emphasizes on the productivity, objectives and goals while making any decisions relating to work. It includes rules, policies, procedures etc. It is the X axis which runs horizontally from left to right of the managerial grid.

The five leadership styles based on the two axes are:

a. Country Club Management (1, 9): In this type of leadership, the concern for people is very high and the concern for production is very low. The work environment is very friendly and oriented towards the welfare of workers. The leaders believe that as long as employees are happy and satisfied, their productivity will increase. This type of leadership exists mainly due to the increased interest in the needs and feelings of employees which result in a lack of direction and control among employees. The leader finds it hard to punish the employees and hence the relationship between the employer & employee becomes very casual, like friends.

b. Impoverished Management (1, 1): In this type of leadership, there is a low concern for people and low concern for production. Leaders don't interact with people nor involve in their job. They merely act as a medium for communication without any interest. The leaders are ineffective and the result of such leadership is disorganization, dissatisfaction, and disharmony. The leader doesn't get any work done from the employees and doesn't put efforts to creating a working atmosphere that motivates employees. It is also referred to as laissez-faire style of leadership.

c. Team Management (9, 9): In this type of leadership, the concern for people and production is very high. The leader is able to strike the right balance between satisfying employee needs and meeting organizational goals. Leaders completely involve in the organization and have full knowledge, ability and skill to motivate employees and get the work. This type of leadership leads to improved performance, low absenteeism, and high job satisfaction. The leader trusts the employees and vice versa, which brings in great harmony between them and leads to higher commitment towards the organization. It is based on Theory Y of McGregor and has been termed as the most effective style of leadership.

d. Authority-Obedience Management (9, 1): This type of leadership has high concern for production and very low concern for people. Such leaders concentrate on the organizational goals, how to develop competitive policies, utilization of resources, quality of work and production etc. It is also called autocratic-task oriented leadership. This style is based on Theory X of McGregor. The leader strongly believes that productivity can be increased only by having the right system in place and supports the elimination of people wherever possible to decrease cost and improve efficiency through technological advancements. They view punishments as the most effective way of motivating employees to work better towards the goals.

e. Organization Man Management (5, 5): They have equal concern for people and production and hence lie in the middle of the managerial grid. The goals set are moderate and achieved through support of the employees. However, it is not an ideal compromise. The leaders settle for average performance and strongly believe that it is the best one could do. This decreases the overall production of the organization. It is also known as "Middle of the road" leadership style. The boundaries of the achievement aren't pushed in this style and which produces average results in the organization. The expectations and needs of employees and the production aren't completely met under this style.

Managerial%20Grid

Pros and Cons of Managerial Grid

Pros:

a. It allows for self-assessment of the leadership style.
b. It is used for training and development of the leaders.

Cons:

a. It doesn't consider internal and external variables.

b. Minimum empirical data to support the study.

3. CONTINGENCY THEORY :

Contingency leadership theory proposes that there is no single way of effective and leadership style should be situational. It propounds that success of a leader is a function of various contingencies in the form of individual, group or task variables. Effectiveness a particular leadership behavior is contingent upon various aspects which impose demands on the situation. Some of the contingency theories of leadership are as follows:

a. Fielders Contingency Model (LPC MODEL) (Focus on the match between the leader's style and the degree to which the situation gives the leader control).

The Contingency Theory leadership was proposed by the Austrian Psychologist Fred Edward Fielder in 1964. This theory emphasizes on both leader's personality and situational factors which affect the leader's operations. He said that there is no one best style of leadership and the effectiveness of a leader depends on the "leadership style" along with the "situational favorableness". The Fielder Model propagates that effective group/team performance depends on upon the match between the leader's style of communicating with the followers and the level to which the situation favors the leader to exercise control and influence.

The two basic assumptions of Fielder's Contingency Theory are:

- Different situations require different styles of leadership
- Leaders do not readily change their leadership style

Fielder measured the leadership through Least Preferred Co-Worker Scale (LPC scale). The LPC questionnaire asks the employees to think of all their co-workers with whom they have ever worked and describe the one they least enjoyed with by rating them on a scale of 1 to 8 for each of 16 sets of adjectives such as pleasant/ unpleasant, efficient/inefficient, open/guarded etc. If a respondent rates an employee with whom he/she is least able to work within favorable terms (High LPC score) then, Fielder labeled them as relationship oriented. If a respondent rates an employee with whom he/she is least able to work within unfavorable terms (Low LPC score) then, Fielder labeled them as task oriented.

Once the LPC score is obtained, the leader's score is matched with the situational factors. As per Fielder, there are three contingency or situational dimensions:

a. Leader-member relations: It is the degree/level to which the members/employees have trust, confidence, and respect towards the leader.

b. Task Structure: It is the degree/level to which the job aspects are structured or unstructured. It emphasizes on task clarity and task accomplishment.

c. Position Power: It is the degree/level to which a leader influences variables such as hiring, firing, discipline, promotions, salary hike etc. The amount of reward or punishment authority that a leader has over his subordinates.

The better the leader-member relations, the more highly structured the job. The stronger the position power, the more control the leader has. This can be explained by the role of payroll manager. A payroll manager is usually well respected by the employees and has confidence in him (leader-member relations). The payroll manager has certain methods and ways of handling the compensation such as computation techniques, tax formats, report making etc. (task structure). He even has the authority to cut the salary of employees for varied reasons such as reporting late to work every day, taking more than assigned number of leaves etc. (positional power). This accounts for a favorable situation. In contrast, an unfavorable situation might be that of a disliked chairperson of a committee which is into fundraising. This would lead to very less control from the leader.

Pros of Fielder's Contingency Model

- There are various empirical studies that have been conducted which supports the contingency model of leadership
- It has broadened the focus on a single, best style of leadership and emphasizes the influence of situational factors.
- It is also said to have "predictive powers" which determines the effectiveness of a leader in various situations.

Cons of Fielder's Contingency Model

- It fails to explain why certain style isn't effective in some situations but not others.
- LPC scale is not very valid and reliable when compared to other standard measures.

- It doesn't explain what needs to be done when there is a mismatch between a leader and a situation in the workplace.

b. Hersey and Blanchard's Situational Leadership Theory (SLT) - Focus is on followers

Situational Leadership Theory was proposed by Paul Hersey and Ken Blanchard in 1970's. It is a part of contingency theories. It propagates that there is no single best leadership style and the leadership is effective when the leadership style matches the readiness of the followers. The followers need to first accept the leader and must have the ability and willingness to complete the task assigned to them.

Choosing the right leadership styles is based upon the readiness of the followers that measure through their willingness and ability. The leaders must choose one of the following behaviors depending upon the follower's readiness:

a. S1 – Telling/Directing: In this, the followers (R1) are unwilling and unable to do the task. There are low commitment and competence from the followers. Hence the leaders need to focus more on the task and give less importance to relationships with the followers. The leader must take a directive role and communicate to the followers to the followers about what needs to be done. A working structure is usually provided to the follower. The leader will also try to find out the reasons for unwillingness and inability and motivate such employees who are less confident. The relationship orientation is not given importance as the followers might get confused about what needs to be done and will lose their direction.

b. S2 –Selling/Coaching: In this, the followers (R2) are willing to do the task but are unable to do due to less competence. There is some competence but variable commitment towards work. The leader must have a high focus on task and relationship. The leaders of this type must display high task orientation to compensate for the lack of the ability of the followers and must also try to "sell" or "get them buy into" the desires of leaders. The directive role might demotivate them or lead to resistance. The leaders need to listen and advise and simultaneously coach the followers to acquire necessary skills.

c. S3 – Participating/Supporting: In this, the followers (R3) have high competence but are unwilling to do the work. There is high competence but commitment is very low. The leader must have less focus on the task and more focus on the relationship. A supportive and participative style of leadership is necessary as the followers need to be motivated and attracted towards doing the work and using their competence. The followers have the skills, ability, and knowledge to complete the task. However, they need to be persuaded to complete the task by creating a friendly environment that promotes the welfare of the followers. The leader need not show them what needs to be done, but must find out why the follower is refusing to do it and motivate them to complete the task.

d. S4 – Delegating/ Observing: In this, the followers (R4) have high competence and high commitment to complete specific tasks. The leader must have low task focus and low relationship focus. The followers in this quadrant are highly motivated to do the job along with excellent capabilities. The leaders should just foresee all the activities and interfere only when it is necessary. The followers usually yearn for frequent praise, recognition etc.

from their leaders. The way in which followers are completing the task must be observed by the leaders. However, the leaders must ensure that followers aren't over-confident about their competence and commitment. The leaders must ensure that progress is made in the work environment.

Pros of Situational Leadership Theory

- It is very simple and easy to apply in the work environment.
- The readiness of the followers is considered as a factor for leader's effectiveness.
- It recognizes the need for flexibility of leader behavior.

Cons of Situational Leadership Theory

- It doesn't consider time constraints and task complexities.
- The other situational factors aren't considered in this theory apart from followers' maturity.
- It doesn't help in predicting future behaviors of the followers.

c. Path-goal model theory

The Path-Goal Theory was first introduced by Martin Evans in 1970 and was further developed by House and Mitchell in 1971. It propagates that the job of a leader is to assist his/her followers in achieving the goals and objectives of an organization. The leaders must give a roadmap which followers could follow, remove all the roadblocks on the path and increase the rewards along the way. The leaders might vary their approach as per situations. During giving a path, they could be directive. While clearing the roadblocks, they could caution the followers and educate how to remove obstacles in future. They could encourage and motivate followers while increasing their rewards.

This theory identifies 4 different leadership behaviors:

a. Supportive Leadership: In this, leader emphasizes a lot on the relationship with the followers. The needs of the follower are considered and adequate guidance is given. Leaders create a friendly atmosphere and improve the self-esteem of the followers. The leader is very sensitive towards the followers. It is the best style to be used when the tasks are repetitive and stressful.

b. Directive Leadership: In this style, the leader focuses on the tasks. The leader communicates the goals and expectations. Tasks are clearly delegated. The followers are instructed as to what needs to be done when and how. Specific work schedules are given with appropriate time schedule. The role ambiguity is decreased through this style. It is the best style to be used when the tasks are unstructured and complex & the members are inexperienced.

c. Participative Leadership: There is a mutual participation between employees and the leaders. The ideas and opinions of the followers are considered while solving problems and making decisions. The employees feel committed to the organization as their views are considered important. It is the best style to be used when the followers are highly experienced and the task is complex.

d. Achievement-oriented Leadership: Leaders set challenging goals for the followers. The leader has high confidence in the abilities of the followers and hence maintains high standards for everyone. Goals set are for self-improvement as well as for the development of the organization. Leaders show faith in the competence and commitment of the followers. This style works best when the followers are not motivated to complete their tasks. Such leadership styles are seen in sales industries.

Leaders are effectively leading the path which the followers would follow. It assumes that the leader knows everything and the followers are dependent upon the leader.

Pros of Path-Goal Theory

- It provides leaders the flexibility to plan according to the requirements.
- It is easy to understand and apply
- The followers are under the guidance of leaders at every stage

Cons of Path-Goal Theory

- It assumes that followers don't know what is good for them
- If the leader himself/herself has flaws, then this method isn't viable
- It is very subjective as leaders decide the method to be used, which may not always be rational.

LEADERSHIP STYLES

Kurt Lewin and his co-researchers at University of Iowa identified three leadership styles:

1. Autocratic Style: It is a classical style of leadership. The manager retains the power within him. The manager is the decision-making authority and doesn't consult employees for the same. The subordinates must follow the orders of the autocratic leaders without questioning them. There are a structured reward and punishment for motivating the employees. To simply put it, "Leader is the boss" in this style. It relies heavily on old beliefs and values. It is usually mistaken as a style which includes yelling, demanding, negative use of power etc. Actually, the leaders are focusing on the task more importantly than the leadership and hence such an attitude is seen. It emphasizes one-way communication. Autocratic leaders have high turnover and absenteeism. However, it is effective during certain situations. Such as:

- To train new employees
- To motivate employees who do not respond to other styles of leadership
- Need for high volume productivity
- Time constraint for decision-making
- An employee challenges the leader's power

However, it shouldn't be used when it creates negative consequences such as fear, resentment, tension, low employee morale etc.

Examples: School teacher, parents are autocratic leaders. Usually, military leaders are also authoritative in nature.

Factories with high volume production will have autocratic leaders.

2. Democratic Style: It is a participative style of leadership. It believes in keeping the employees informed about the happenings. The problem solving and decision making is shared with the subordinates. A democratic leader welcomes inputs and facilitates group discussion so that employees feel important in the organization. The leaders follow a "Coach style" who takes the final decision after considering the views of the subordinates. Democratic leaders offer multiple options to the subordinates which broaden the wavelength of the employees in a positive manner. They allow for multiple viewpoints and participation from the employees. However, the leader maintains influence and control. Each member's strength is recognized by a participative leader and he/she encourages employees to do their best. They allow the employees to establish goals and work towards them. It recognizes and rewards employees as they can produce large quantity with quality production for a long period of time. It is used in various situations such as:

- It is important to use when the employees need to be kept informed.
- To encourage and motivate employees in decision-making
- It used to solve complex problems which require multiple perspectives
- To promote team building and participation.
- To assist employees in meeting their organizational and personal goals and support their growth in the organization.

It shouldn't be used as there is a time constraint. The business can't afford to make mistakes and hence the leaders should be alert to understand the pulse of the employees.

Example: Indian Government acts as a democratic body which involves all the citizens while making decisions. It also allows foreign citizens to voice their opinions about the Government.

3. Laissez Faire: It is the hands-off approach of leadership. The leadership responsibilities are shared by all the members. It is very useful in businesses where creative ideas are very important. The members have a control over their work life and hence can be highly motivational. However, it relies on good teamwork and interpersonal relations. A major drawback of this approach is that it could make the decision making a time-consuming process which would eventually lead to a loss of direction. The communication between leaders and members is widespread but needs a base. Such leaders don't give proper direction to the subordinates and allow them to set goals on their own. The leader acts as an umpire and doesn't involve much in the work.

Paternalistic Leaders: The leader acts like a "Father Figure" to the members. The relationship between the elders and the subordinates is the same as between the head of the family and the other members of the family. The leader will make the final decision but may consult the members. It believes the need to support staff members and hence takes care of them like a father. It is a softer form of authoritarian leadership and it results in increased motivation and low turnover. It might not be successful in every situation as some of them don't like to be addressed as godfather. It might lead to resentment and antagonism.

CUTTING EDGE APPROACHES TO LEADERSHIP

In today's world, leadership is vital at every stage. The drive to do a work, complete a project, take decisions etc. depends on upon the leadership qualities. There are four approaches to leadership which are becoming increasingly important in today's scenario.

1. Transactional Leadership (the 1970s) : This is also known as " Exchange theory " of leadership. It is characterized by the transactions made by the leader and follower and hence the name. This type of leadership is used when the leaders are heavily focused on the task. They need to motivate their followers by providing them direction to achieve established goals. They clearly mention all the role expectations and job requirements. The focus is on completing the job successfully. It is concerned with maintaining the normal flow of activities in the workplace. It is best described as "Keeping the ship afloat." They use discipline and rewards to motivate employees towards the work. Such leaders do not foresee any changes to be made in the future as the focus is only on today. It is called transactional because the reward or punishment is based on the performance of the subordinate. Transactional leaders motivate employees by appealing to their self-interest and fulfillment of such interests.

2. Transformational Leader: (the 1970s) Transformational Leaders inspire their followers to go beyond their own self-interests for the betterment of the organization. Such leaders have a profound effect on their followers. They are proactive in nature and empower employees by motivating them to achieve organizational objectives. They go beyond the day-to-day requirements of an organization and work towards the next level of performances or success. They provide space for personal growth of the employees. The goals of the self and the group/unit are integrated by such leaders and they support the group at every level. Richard Branson of the Virgin Group is a transformational leader as he developed the interest in the development of employees along with the group. The CEO of China Mobile – Wang Jianzohu is a transformational leader who inspires his employees to excel in their work . With the help of such motivated workforce , he is expanding the mobile service through the rural areas and plans to expand in emerging markets such as Africa, Asia, and Latin America.

3. Charismatic Leader: Charismatic leaders have an attractive personality which influences people to behave in a particular way. They are enthusiastic and self-confident. They have a vision, articulate the vision, take risks to achieve the vision, sensitive towards the needs of the environment and are extraordinary in their behaviors. The aura of such leaders is contagious and hence it binds all the followers towards the leader. It results in increased motivation, improved satisfaction, more profits etc. Through charismatic leadership, positive correlation between satisfaction and performance of the employees could be observed. Barack Obama, Herb Kelleher of South West Airlines, GE's Jack Welch, Madonna etc. are some of the charismatic leaders.

4. Visionary Leader: This type of leader has a long sighted vision which is articulated in a manner that positively affects the present situation. Their vision is realistic, credible and attractive. The visionary leaders explain their vision to others through words and behavior and apply it in various contexts of leadership. It goes beyond the charisma of a person and concentrates on the special skills of a leader. The vision ensures that abilities, talent, skills etc. of individuals are utilized to the utmost extent in order to achieve the vision. These leaders visualize their vision being fulfilled by tapping the emotions and energies of the subordinates. They build enthusiasm among people to work towards the vision. A.G. Lafley is a visionary and a transformational leader who joined P&G in as a CEO in 2000. He has introduced a lot of flexibility and creativity in the company. With more than half of P&G's business being outside the USA, he recast the top management group with Non-Americans up to 50%. These changes have improved the revenues of P&G.

I look up to Dhoni's leadership skills for inspiration: Jason Holder – The Economic Times – May 26, 2015

"MS is an influential figure. In true sense, he is a leader and I found that during my stint with Chennai Super Kings in the Indian Premier League. As a captain, I have always looked up to MS's leadership qualities for inspiration. The manner in which Dhoni handles pressure is exceptional. That is the reason he has achieved so much while leading a team with players from different countries. There is so much to learn from him." – **West Indies Captain – Jason Holder.**

CURRENT LEADERSHIP ISSUES

Even though there are contemporary leadership styles to suit the current requirements, there are many leadership issues which hurdle the smooth functioning of the organization.

a. Managing Power: The leaders are using their positional power negatively to influence employees which is not in support of the organization.

b. The credibility of a Leader: The leaders' qualities need to be assessed so that the followers could strongly believe the leader. Nowadays, the leader's qualities keep changing as per the surroundings that personally benefit them.

c. Trust – It is very important for the leader to believe the followers and vice versa. However, in today's competitive world, the integrity, character, ability of a leader is always questioned.

CLOSING CASE

Who Makes A Better Leader: A Man Or A Woman? – Forbes - 23/07/2014

In 2012, women held just 3.8% of Chief Executive Officer Positions in Fortune 500 companies, and 90 out of 535 seats in US Congress. Much has been written about why women are so severely underrepresented in senior leadership – from poor childcare provisions to institutional bias. One thing researchers can't agree on is whether there are fewer women leaders because they're less effective at the job, or because society expects them to be.

One theory goes that society generally associates successful leadership with stereotypically 'masculine' traits such as assertiveness and dominance, and so disapproves of female leaders because they violate these gender norms. As a result, women experience greater obstacles to reaching the upper echelons. In the 1970s Virginia Schein came up with the phrase 'think manager-think male' to explain the automatic association between leadership and masculinity – an association which still exists, in certain circumstances, today. But with the recent rise of transformational leadership and its emphasis on traditionally 'feminine' traits like empathy, collaboration, and emotional intelligence, could the expectations of female leaders be shifting?

Of course, there is no universal rule: different individuals are differently suited to different situations, and context is, as ever, king. To that end, a study published recently in the Journal of Applied Psychology aimed to add a more nuanced insight to the 'male vs female leaders' debate. By analyzing the results of 99 different studies that measured leaders' effectiveness from 1962 to 2011, the researchers were able to unpick the situations in which male or female leaders excelled.

Perhaps unsurprisingly, the results suggested that the culture of the organization makes a difference: in traditionally male-dominated, masculine organizations like government or the military, male leaders were more effective, while women triumphed in more 'feminine' environments like social services and education. Interestingly, under the vague umbrella term 'business', female leaders also came out on top.

What's more, the results also highlighted that it matters who you ask. When leaders rated their own effectiveness, men tended to rate themselves higher than women. But when other people (peers, bosses, subordinates or third-party observers) did the rating, women were seen as significantly more effective than men – particularly in studies from 1982 and later. This was especially true taking into account the different levels of leadership: at lower, supervisor levels, men rated themselves higher than women, while women were seen by others to be more effective in mid- and upper-level positions.

There are a few possible explanations for this pattern of results:

a. The recent trend towards transformational leadership and its emphasis on empowerment and collaboration – traits traditionally associated with women – means that leadership is increasingly seen as a domain more suited to women.

b. Because of the many obstacles that women experience on their way to the top and the assumption that management is better suited to males, people assume that women who have made it to a mid- or high-level management position must be extra special, and so credit them with elevated competence ('she must be really good to have made it that far').

c. Men have an over-inflated view of their own ability and women really do make better leaders.

Perhaps the most important result from this meta-analysis was that taking into account self and other ratings, across all types of organizations and all leadership levels, there was no significant difference between male and female leaders. Perhaps in 2014, it's time we all looked further than gender and concentrated instead on which skills make the best leaders – male or female

Source:http://www.forbes.com/sites/sebastianbailey/2014/07/23/who-makes-a-better-leader-a-man-or-a-woman/

CHAPTER THREE

BUSINESS PROCESS OUTSOURCING

Meaning

BPO stands for Business Process Outsourcing. BPO in a general term used to describe the outsourcing of critical, but non-core, business processes or functions of an organization to external vendors for certain period on a set of predefined performance metrices.

It is the contracting of a specific business task, such as payroll, to a third-party service provider. BPO is handing over a particular Business Process to a Third Party Service Provider.

For example a Company whose primary business is to manufacture and sell computers might hire a Company to handle calls of it's customers for servicing and repair works.

In this case the Company which is handling the incoming calls of customers is a nothing but a BPO Company which is taking up a process of another company.

BPO is typically categorised into Back Office outsourcing - which may include business functions like Human Resource, Finance, Accounting, Email etc and Front Office outsourcing - which may include Customer Service,

Complaints, Contact Center etc.

Benefits of BPO –

The Outsourcing market is growing tremendously in the coming few with increasing years with an increasing advantage as discussed below:-

1. Productivity improvement:

BPO enables to the corporate executive to concentrate upon core business areas. Conventionally executives spend more time in management of details and they get very little time to formulate strategies. BPO saves time and helps the executives to explore new revenue areas, accelerate other projects and focus on their customers. This leads to improvement in the productivity. Better educated or skilled people perform the task efficiently and thus improve productivity.

2. Optimum utilisation of the resources:

BPO enables optimum utilisation of resources of scarce resources. Outsourcing helps to capture new efficiencies and reallocate the resources. This increases the efficiency and productivity. Availability of skilled employees and adoption of sophisticated technologies leads to utilisation of resources and productivity.

3. Reduction in cost:

Cost savings can be significant to any business. BPO not only helps in reducing cost but also increase productivity and raise revenue significantly. Cost reduction is possible through process improvements, reengineering, and use of technologies that reduce and bring administrative and other costs under control. Outsourcing helps the company maintain lower rates with better service solutions, thereby giving them a better market position and even a competitive advantage.

4. Improved Human Resource:

Improved HR is another great advantage of outsourcing business processes. Cost effective manpower is yet another important factor of importance in BPO. Companies today, require productive and efficient human resource that can generate economies of scale. Due to outsourcing business can save Human resource cost, depending on their priorities. Outsourcing gives a company the ability to get access to skilled and trained man power at extremely low rates

5. Focus on core business areas:

Efficient business strategy is essential to take the business to the top. Outsourcing enables the top management level to hand over critical but non-core activities of the business to the third party. This facilitates top management level to concentrate on the core activities.

6. Cater to changing customer demands:

It is another great advantage of outsourcing the business processes. Many BPOs provide the management with flexible services to meet the customers' changing requirements, and to support company acquisitions, consolidations, and joint ventures.

7. Sophisticated technology at lower cost:

Technology is the leading area of outsourcing. It makes much of the work of modern organisation easy. Investing in new technology is very costly and often risky. As the technology market develops rapidly, it is difficult to keep pace with the latest innovations and solutions. Thus outsourcing to companies that have the resources, expertise and desire to continuously update their technological solutions, offers a true advantage of outsourcing.

Service providers who undertake the responsibility of performing such activities can either offer only few of the outsourcing activities or a more end to end services encompassing of much larger range of activities. This depends on the capabilities developed by such BPO vendors and the scale at which the vendor operates.

BPO services have three kinds of business model depending on the type of activities handled by them. These are as follows:

1. Transactional
2. Niche and
3. Comprehensive

Transactional: Transactional providers typically handle only one process and not the entire activity. They are at the low end of the value chain.

For example: In Payroll, the BPO vendors will not take over the entire department but will be responsible for only one activity, like cutting cheques.

Such contracts are short generally annual or less than 2 years. And have less contract value. Performance metrics are decided per transaction and the company has total control over the whole process and has to develop an in-house department to monitor it. Generally occurs in initial stages of BPO.

Niche: Niche providers handle a wider range or sequence of transactions, typically 2 or 4 processes. But they still don't handle the entire activity. These deals tend to be 3 or more years. And the contract value is also more than the transactional providers. They have good domain knowledge and are also effect productivity and quality improvements over a period of time. They aim to make selected processes more efficient by lowering costs for the companies and raising service levels.

Comprehensive: Comprehensive providers handle almost all the transactional and administrative processes in a function.

For example: Handling of entire HR function – which includes all the 22 activities.

They are typically long term contracts, 10 yrs and look for global deals. The value of this type of contract is very high and goes in billions of dollars. Comprehensive vendors have ability to make interrelated functions more efficient by introducing best practices, thereby reducing the total cost of a function. They are completely responsible and accountable for the entire function.

Example – Exult (since acquired by HP)

Interestingly, Transactional services providers act as sub contractors for Niche service providers and both act as sub-contractors to Comprehensive service providers. They effectively act as Tier III, Tier II and Tier I outsourcers.

BPO vendors can be classified into three distinct types depending on the history or origin of the company, expertise etc.

1. Traditional IT services/IT Outsourcing companies: these companies have a good track of services in traditional IT areas. Companies such as IBM, Global Services, Unisys, Infosys, Wipro, TCS etc fall into this category. They have started offering their expertise and client relationships that are already in existence.
2. Consulting firms: these companies have distinct advantage of working with several companies and are hence exposed to the best practices followed worldwide. They also help in re-engineer processes and helps in

reducing cost. Their domain knowledge gives them tremendous competitive advantage to build CEO level relationships over a period of time. Companies such as Hewitt, Accenture, Ernst and young are come consulting firms.

3. Pure Play BPO Vendors: these companies are setup exclusively for undertaking BPO contracts. Such companies have grown over a period of time relatively lower end Transaction BPO and Niche BPOs. The growth is in the areas like transcription, call centre's, e-accounts etc.

Healthcare BPO

Healthcare BPO industry involves outsourcing activities related to creation, maintenance and exchange of patient information between healthcare providers (Hospitals, Physicians, clinics, Pharmacies etc) and the healthcare payers such as insurance companies. Some of the healthcare services include

Medical transcription: conversion of medical data from speech or handwritten format to electronic form

Document management: Collation of patients' medical and demographic record into a single computerized patient record with database and e-signature functionalities.

Coding: Assigning the predefined diagnostic and treatment codes to different medical procedures

Billing: Combining patient records, codes and charge sheets to generate claims/bills.

Form processing: scanning of handwritten documents, converting them into electronic form and sending it back.

Receivable management: Follow-up and collection of receivables.

Company health analysis: medical history of all employees of a company is analyzed to find out the health risk of a company.

List of some MT companies in India:

CBay Systems, Healthscribe, Heartland, Microgenetics, Saral Infotech, Medsoft, Mediscribe etc.

Transaction Processing BPO

Most of the organizations around the world face the tedious task of processing countless transaction to record day to day activities that they perform in the process of providing goods and services to their customers. They need to generate, manage and document multiple forms in an organized, accessible manner. They then need to process the data according to a set of pre-defined rules, often with the use of computers. Output data from one process acts as the input data for another process. This series of rule based data processing is called transaction processing.

Transaction processing includes Banking transactions, credit and card processing, mortgage processing, claims processing and horizontal areas like basic accounting, receivables management, accounts payables etc.

Companies outsource these activities which are repetitive and they can in turn focus on enhancing their core competencies and serving their customers better.

Some of the reasons why companies prefer outsourcing such transactions intensive activities are :

- This high cost of transactions
- Too much time spent on daily operations
- The high cost of upgrading applications
- Difficulty in hiring and retaining the high quality process staff

- Inability to put best practices and performance parameters in place.

Human Resource BPO

The HR department is critical for employee well-being in any business no matter how small the business is. A motivated and innovative employee can work wonders for a marketplace. HR outsourcing is defined as the process of outsourcing the HR activities to a third party having expertise in HR field.

The typical services include:

- Payroll administration: producing cheques, handling taxes, dealing with sick time and vacation time
- Employee benefits: Health and medical life, 401(k) plans, cafeteria etc
- HR management: Recruiting, hiring and firing, background interviews, exit and wage interviews
- Risk Management: Workers' compensation, dispute resolution, safety inspection, Office policies and handbooks.

Offshoring

Many corporations in the developed countries did not feel that the cost of benefit of outsourcing to a service provider located in their own country was not worth their while. The following terms are used to indicate the location of the service providers

1. Onshore: In case the service provider is located on the shore i.e if the US based company is outsourcing to another US based company, the process will be called onshoring.

2. Near-shoring: In case the service provider is located near the shore in a lower cost country location in nearby countries. For example: if a US based company outsources to another company based in Canada, the process is called near shoring.
3. Off shore: In case the service provider is located far away from the company which is outsourcing work and the communication and control is exerted using IT enable tools over long distance telecom networks. For example: if a US based company outsources work to another company based in India, the process is called offshoring.

The dominant role in the birth of offshoring can be credited to rise of Information Technology, reduction in networking costs and internet. Offshoring in the manufacturing industry accelerated in a big way with two events. The first event was the signing of NAFTA (North American Free Trade Agreement) in 1993, which gave boost to the process of offshoring. The second event was 1994 passage of GATT (General Agreement on Trade and Tariffs) further accelerated its opened door policy towards investment and a new aspect of outsourcing emerged.

Many multinational companies preferred to outsource work to India and other Asian Countries such as Philippines, Malaysia etc. since they offered unique combination of low costs and quality manpower.

BPO in India

Due to the open market and the demand for outsourcing, more and more BPO companies in India are setting up bases in various parts of the country. Most of these companies cater to the global MNCs, banks and so on. The business process outsourcing sector is one of the booming industries in the country and more and more young professionals are joining it to earn good salary.

According to the recent surveys, the BPO industry provides employment to around 0.7 million people across the country. The yearly revenue amounts to around $11 billion with a share of around 1 % of the annual Gross Domestic Product (GDP). The BPO industry is also a lucrative option for both graduates and freshers as one can get good salary. The growth rate of the wages and salaries in the sector range from 10-15 % every year.

There are also well known domestic BPO companies which cater to the national as well as the international market. Some of the cities where the business processing industry is popular are Chennai, Bangalore, Hyderabad, Kolkata, New Delhi, and Mumbai and so on. To cater to the growing demand, more BPO companies are also setting up bases in other cities across the country like Pune, Gurgaon, Coimbatore, Kochi, Chandigarh, Bhubaneshwar, and Lucknow and so on.

Leading BPO companies in India

The BPO companies are judged according to the clients they cater to, their work and the output and also the employee welfare and satisfaction. Based on these, some of the well known BPO companies are:

Genpact: Established in the year 1997, Genpact conducts a major portion of the outsourcing services in India. It offers outsourcing operations for big companies like GE Capital. Genpact has around 30 branches all across the globe and offers excellent services in the field of accounting and finance, customer service, insurance, analytics, IT infrastructure and so on. The company has staff strength of around 34,000 employees with revenue of around $822.7 million.

Daksh eServices: Ranking among the fastest growing BPO companies in India, Daksh has employee strength of around 5000. It offers high standard solutions in customer care and back office analytics. Some of the specialized departments include Technical Support, Customer Care, and Transaction Processes. In the year 2004, Daksh was taken over by IBM.

ICICI OneSource: ICICI OneSource specializes in providing solutions to various sectors such as healthcare, media, publishing, finance, and telecom. Recent surveys have shown that around 4500 people work in the company. The company has also received the BS 7799 certification.

EXL Services: EXL Services has its offices in Noida and Pune. It employs around 5000 employees and is a well known name among the BPO companies in India. It offers high quality services in mortgage lending, banking, health care, insurance, collections, and analytics. It has been awarded the prestigious ISO 9001:2000 certification for its quality performance.

HCL-Tech BPO: A subsidiary company of HCL Technologies, HCL-Tech BPO has around 3000 employees and offers cutting edge services in customer care, back office processing and so on. It has four centers in Bangalore, Chennai and Noida.

CHAPTER FOUR

MOTIVATION

Motivation

Among all the factors of production, human resource is the most important factor due to the reason that when all other resources are the same, productivity can be greatly altered by altering the human factor. Motivation is the concept employed in altering the performance of an employee by varied means to fulfill certain organizational objectives. A motivated employee gives the best possible performance which is beneficial for the organization. Similarly, a demotivated group of employees can impede the growth of an organization.

The word Motivation is derived from the Latin movere, which means "to move".

Motivation is a psychological phenomenon which is generated within an individual. Employee performance can be predicted by the level of motivation of employees. The following formula gives the connection between motivation and employee performance:

Performance = f(Ability* Motivation)

The components of motivation as described by Arnold are Direction – what a person is trying to do, Effort – how hard a person is trying, Persistence

– how long a person keeps on trying to do what is expected out of him.

Definition of motivation

According to Vance, 'Motivation implies any emotion or desire which so conditions one's will that the individual is properly led into action.'

According to Dubin, 'Motivation is the complex of forces starting and keeping a person at work in an organization

Nature of Motivation

Motivation is an inner feeling that makes the person work more. It is concerned with channelizing the employee effort towards achieving organization objectives and missions. Every individual needs some form of motivation. It is a continuous and complex process. Motivation produces target-directed behaviour.

2 types of factors that influence motivation are:

Intrinsic –They are the self-generated factors (responsibility, autonomy, scope to use and develop skills and abilities, attractive and challenging work, opportunities for progression etc). In comparison to extrinsic factors, they have a deeper and longer-term effect on the behavior of employees.

Extrinsic - These are the factors which are outside the realm of the job by itself. It includes those what is done for people to motivate them (rewards, promotion, punishment). Extrinsic factors have an instant and potent effect but are not long lasting.

Importance of Motivation

1. Motivation brings out untapped energies, both mental and physical.

2. It brings down the cost of production by increasing employee efficiency.

3. Motivation boosts novelty and creativity in thinking

4. It reduces absenteeism and employee turnover by improving loyalty towards the organization.

5. When the employees are motivated in the organization, it improves the image of the organization and improves employer branding.

6. Finally, an organization with motivated employees will have better and harmonious industrial relations.

Types of Motivation

Positive motivation: This deals with motivating the workforce with positive motivation techniques like promotions, augmented pay, providing fringe benefits, ESOPS, recreation facility etc. These methods are aimed at improving employee's performance.

*Negative Motivatio*n: In negative motivation, the employees are motivated by using negative motivation techniques like punishments, demotions, pay cut, punishment transfers etc. The idea behind using negative motivation is to make the employees realize that their performance is not on par with the organization's expectations so that they work towards improving their performance.

Financial motivators: The economists advocate financial motivators as the most potential motivators. It includes increased wage and salary, bonus, other fringe benefits etc. The importance of money as a strong motivator was emphasized by many traditional management thinkers like Abraham Maslow, Herzberg, and Alderfer. Money as a motivator acts better with young employees, who may have young children whom they may have to educate and those who have much more financial commitments.

Non–financial motivators: Nonfinancial motivators take the form of better status in the organization, recognition, participation in decision making, job security etc.

Ways of motivating employees in an organization

We can broadly classify the ways of motivating employees into 4 categories. There are many theories of motivation which fall under each category. Let us examine those categories and their respective theories.

1. Motivating employees through meeting human needs
a. Need hierarchy theory of Maslow
b. Achievement model of McClelland
c. ERG theory of motivation by Alderfer
2. Motivating employees through job design
a. Two Factor Theory of Herzberg
3. Motivating employees through performance expectations
a. Expectancy and Valence Theory by Victor Vroom
4. Motivating employees through equity
a. Equity Theory by Adam.
5. Contemporary theories of motivation
a) Goal Setting Theory
b) Self-efficacy Theory
c) Equity

d) Expectancy
e) Reinforcement

1. a) Abraham H. Maslow's need hierarchy theory:

Clinical psychologist Abraham Maslow propounded the theory of the hierarchy of needs. According to him, people have a complex set of unmet and exceptionally strong needs and these sets of needs can be arranged in a hierarchy. It is assumed in this theory that once the unmet need is fulfilled, its motivational importance declines and the next set of needs emerge. As per the theory, lower sets of needs should be met before considering higher level needs. The theory divides the set of needs into 5 groups viz physiological, safety/security, affiliation, esteem/ego and self-actualization. Maslow classified physiological and safety needs as lower level needs and affiliation, esteem and self-actualization as a higher order of needs. Higher level needs are satisfied internally whereas a lower level of needs is met by external means. Following are examples of different levels of needs in the hierarchy:

1. *Physiological needs* - Include hunger, thirst, air, shelter, sex, sleep, etc.

2. *Safety needs* - Include absence of pain, fear, protection from unfavourable events, and protection from other emotional and physical harm.

3. *Affiliation/Social needs:* These include acceptance, friendship, love, work group, family, affection, relationships, etc.

4. *Esteem needs* - These include self-respect, autonomy, achievement, recognition, mastery, status, attention, dominance, prestige, designation etc.

5. *Self-Actualization needs* - These include the drive to reach one's full potential, self-fulfillment, seeking personal growth, challenging assignments etc.

Maslow's need hierarchy is well accepted by practicing managers due to its simplicity and logical application. This suggests types of behaviours to fulfill different levels of needs. Managers need to satisfy higher level needs whereas assembly level workers need to satisfy more of the lower level of needs. This theory suggests that rewarding an employee with the same kind of motivator may have diminished importance in motivating an employee, as the perceived value of the same kind of motivator diminishes after that particular set of needs are fulfilled .

1. b) Achievement Theory by McClelland

David McClelland proposed the "Learned Needs" model of motivation. This theory has particular relevance to industrial enterprises, as an achievement in itself has maximum importance for success or failure of an enterprise.

McClelland postulated that every individual has three particularly important needs: Need for Achievement, Affiliation, and Power. This could vary in degree between individuals. Of the three needs, McClelland focused maximum on nAch.

Need for Achievement (nAch) : It is the need to achieve, drive to stand out, and strive to succeed.

Need for Power (nPow) : This is the need to make other people behave in a way you want them to.

Need for Affiliation (nAff) : It is the need for a friendly and pleasant interpersonal relationship.

Employees with high nAch will perform better when they perceive that their probability of success is at least 50%. They dislike mundane jobs. They select moderate goals which are neither too easy nor too difficult to attain. They set their own goals and like the challenge of making tough decisions. They undertake calculated risk taking and they get achievement satisfaction when they stretch themselves a little to achieve a relatively difficult goal. If they achieve the goal , they want the credit for the same and if they lose, they are ready to accept the blame. They prefer tasks which provide immediate feedback. For them, goals are very important and they want to know whether they are doing well and hence seek feedback for their goal-directed activity. They are aware of their abilities and limitations and they value their services to an organization and charge them accordingly. They are less likely to stick to an organization which does not pay them well. They value money as a symbol of their efficiency and achievement.

High nAchs generally tend to be low in affiliation (nAff). To measure achievement motivation, McClelland used Thematic Apperception Test (TAT) as it catches the pre-conscious motives of the people.

1. c) ERG Theory of Alderfer

Maslow's Need Hierarchy Theory was reworked by Clayton Alderfer to synchronize it with empirical research. Clayton Alderfer redefined need hierarchy theory and formed the needs into three core groups : Existence (Physiological and safety needs of Maslow), Relatedness (Social needs of Maslow), and Growth (Self-esteem and Self-actualization needs of Maslow). This modified theory of Alderfer is known as ERG theory of motivation.

- *Existence needs*- These include the need for fundamental material necessities as in the case of physiological and physical safety needs.

- *Relatedness needs-* These include the individual's need for maintaining good interpersonal relationships with family, peers or superiors, getting public recognition and fame etc. Maslow's social needs and external component of esteem needs form this class of need.
- *Growth needs-* These include the need for personal development, growth and advancement. Maslow's self-actualization needs and intrinsic component of esteem needs form this category of need.

How do you satisfy ERG needs?

Existence : Existence need can be met by providing basic amenities like good lighting and ventilation in the workplace, drinking water, sanitary facilities, canteen, job security, insurance, health programs, time off etc

Relatedness need : This can be met by providing good teamwork, quality supervision, social events etc

Growth needs : This can be fulfilled by providing challenging jobs, autonomy, interesting work, participation in decision making etc.

Unlike Maslow, Alderfer never assumed that the need hierarchy was rigid and that it was not necessary for one set of need to get satisfied, to go to the next set of needs. All three categories of needs may co-exist simultaneously.

2. Frederick Herzberg's Two Factor Theory/ Motivation-Hygiene Theory

Herzberg and associates considered two different approaches while considering the factors that affect the motivation of employees. Research was conducted with a large group of employees and they were asked what they felt were the exceptionally good things about their job and what they felt were exceptionally bad things about their jobs. From the exhaustive list provided by the employees, Herzberg developed two categories and formed

Two Factor Theory which is also known as *Motivator – Hygiene* theory. One category consistently related to job satisfaction while the other consistently related to job dissatisfaction. Employees who are satisfied in the job listed intrinsic factors like recognition, advancement, responsibility, achievement etc. Dissatisfied employees listed extrinsic factors like pay, supervision, working conditions, rules and regulations etc. The theory postulates that two sets of factors - *Motivators* and *Hygiene* are responsible for job satisfaction and job dissatisfaction.

Motivator factors:

Intrinsic job-related factors like the work itself, recognition, career advancement, responsibility, and authority etc form the motivator factors. They are largely internal to the individual. They provide job satisfaction to the employees. These factors motivate the employees to perform better and improve their loyalty to the company. They have a long lasting effect on employees.

Motivating Factors are:-

1. Achievement
2. Appreciation for achievement
3. Increased accountability
4. Opportunity for Growth and advancement
5. Creative and challenging Work

Hygiene Factors:

These factors prevent employees from dissatisfaction but their presence is not motivating. The hygiene factors help employees to avoid unpleasantness but do not motivate them to take more interest in the work. When hygiene factors are provided, it creates a positive environment for motivation and prevents job dissatisfaction. They are largely extrinsic in nature and they are related to job/work conditions. When an employer does not provide sufficient hygiene factors, it leads to employee dissatisfaction. However, if they are provided, they do not guarantee job satisfaction. Some of the hygiene factors are as noted below.

1. Company's HR policies
2. Supervision
3. Working environment
4. Interpersonal relations with colleagues, subordinates, and superiors
5. Salary
6. Job Security

Motivators instill a sense of motivation among employees to work better. Motivators improve the efficiency and productivity of employees. Frederick Herzberg believed that motivators are essential to provide job satisfaction. It also helps in maintaining a high level of job performance.

3. Victor Vroom's Expectancy/ VIE Theory

Valence is the degree of preference of an individual towards an expected outcome. Valence is hence the amount of value an individual perceives in a particular outcome. Valence is more than one or positive when an individual prefers an outcome. When the individual is indifferent about the outcome, the valence is zero.

Instrumentality is the extent or degree to which the first level outcome is likely to bring second level outcome.

Expectancy is the probability that a particular action will lead to the desired outcome. It ranges from 0 to 1. If an individual finds zero probability of an action bringing in the desired outcome, he won't put in an effort to take the action.

Expectancy relates to the effort to be put to get the first level outcome whereas Instrumentality relates first level outcome to second level outcome.

For example, if an employee desires promotion, depending on the strength of desire to get the promotion (Valence), he may perform well thinking high performance will get him a promotion (Expectancy). Importance or weightage of high performance in getting the promotion is instrumentality.

According to the VIE theory, an individual will weigh the 3 aspects before he decides to put an effort to achieve a particular target.

4. Stacy Adams' Equity Theory

This theory stems from the sense of people's justice and fairness. All workers seek a fair balance between the effort put in a job and what we obtain out of it. Adam referred these as inputs and outputs. Inputs, in this context, are an employee's educational qualification, experience, special skill sets etc. Outputs are salary, bonus, benefits, designation, recognition etc.

According to the Equity Theory, a person's motivation depends on the degree of equity that they perceive in the work situation. Perception of fairness will be often based

on the comparison of our own situation in terms of inputs and outputs with other 'referents' (reference points or examples) in the organization. Employees are influenced by contemporaries, friends, and partners in the organization while establishing certain benchmarks. Employees regularly compare their input-output ratio with the input-output ratios of relevant others. The comparison may also extend to other organizations for similar jobs. When an employee perceives inequity in input out ratios of self and others, "equity tension" occurs which creates anger and tension in the individual, leading to resentment. The extent of demotivation is proportional to the perceived inequality between inputs and the expected outputs. When he perceives that he is over-rewarded for his effort, it may lead to guilt. Equity tension motivates a person to correct it. This is done by an under-rewarded person reducing the quantity or quality of output and reducing his commitment to the job and the organization. An over-rewarded person will either work hard to compensate the feeling of guilt or discount the value of the extra reward to maintain balance.

This theory highlights the value of social comparison in motivation. It also recognizes the role of cognitive processes in motivation.

What should be the managerial actions to keep employees motivated in the organization?

- Endow the employee with more valued rewards according to the employee needs and perceived value. For example, establish a suitable reward and incentive system keeping in mind the needs of the majority of employees.
- Change the values of the person towards available rewards. For example, if the company gives group

rewards or team-based pay, often seen in the case of a project in IT companies, consider educating the employees on benefits of group rewards so as to bring in a change in their value system.

- Improve the employees' perception of the linkage between behavior and reward. This can be done by casual conversation with the employees about what could be the probable outcome of a particular level of performance like a pay hike, promotion etc.
- Impress on the employees the reality of the behaviour-reward association. Employees should be made aware of the paying capacity of the organization. In the case of the inability to pay according to market standards, employees should be informed about when in the future they will be rewarded accordingly.

5. a) Goal Setting Theory

Goal-Setting Theory of motivation was proposed by Edwin Locke in late 1960s. This theory lies on the basic principle that goal setting is essentially linked to task performance. It explains that if specific and challenging goals are set with the required feedback from the members of the organization, the organizational activities can be successfully executed and excelled.

Goals give direction to the efforts of the employees. The hard work of the employees could be measured by comparing it with the current scenario with the expected results (goals). One of the main features of the Goal Setting Theory is the willingness of the employees towards the attainment of the goal set by the organization which leads to increased productivity and improved performance.

Goal Setting Theory has certain conditions which ensure that goals are effective, which motivates the employees towards its achievement.

- Goal Acceptance/Goal Commitment: First stage of the goal setting is that the employee must accept the goal. Two important factors that improve goal commitment are the importance of the goal and self-efficacy. The employee needs to understand the positive outcome of attaining the goal and its importance for the development of the organization. Self-efficacy is the belief that they can achieve the set goals. These two factors increase their acceptance level of the goals and in turn improve their goal commitment.
- Goal Specificity: A goal should be specific and to the point. Goals must be- Specific; Measurable; Attainable; Realistic; Time-bound. Ex: The goals of the sales executives of the sales department are to increase the sale of product X by 10% within December 2015. The more specific the goal is, the more explicitly the performance will be affected. It gives a meaning to the goal as employees can track their progress by comparing it with the specific goals.
- Goal Difficulty: The goals must be set high enough to encourage and motivate the employees to reach the goal and low enough to accomplish the goals. A study by Ordonez and Schweitzer (2004) says that people have a tendency to be dishonest if they fall short of their goals. Ex: At Sears, Roebuck and Co., the mechanics engaged in unfair business practices by charging extra to customers and performing repairs that were unneeded just to meet their sales targets. Goals which are too easy might lead to negligence and decreased performance. In

contrast, goals which are very difficult to attain might result in unacceptable behavior. Hence goals need to be moderately difficult which maintains their motivation level to achieve the goals.

- Feedback: Feedback is necessary to ensure that the efforts made towards setting the goals and attaining them are in the right direction. Two types of feedback need to be taken. Process feedback would provide specific tasks that need to perform in order reach the desired outcome. Outcome feedback should be obtained to check whether the proposed goal and attained goal match or not.

Application of motivation theories in the organizational context

1. Leverage the Maslow's need hierarchy by instituting employee recognition programs to satisfy the esteem and self-actualization needs of managers. For meeting the physiological needs of shop floor employees by giving break for lunch and tea. Provision of good safety and security practices like security guards, CCTV camera etc will make employees feel safe at the workplace. Social needs of employees can be met by having team activities and other social events in the workplace.

2. ERG Theory can be effectively used by fixing challenging tasks for employees with high nAch i.e., employees with high achievement motivation so that they feel satisfied in the job. The ERG Theory follows frustration- regression principle. According to this principle, if the higher order of needs like growth needs, are left unfulfilled, the employee may regress to lower level

of needs, which may be relatively easier to satisfy. For example, if the high achiever's growth needs are suppressed, he will regress to lower level need of socializing with colleagues more often than needed and wastes his time. Early warning signals of losing such a star employee should be identified by the management and the need to provide for his growth needs for retention of such employees should be undertaken.

3. As per the Expectancy Theory, employees will put an effort in work commensurate to the perceived value of a reward. Hence use a mixed bag of traditional and contemporary compensation strategies to motivate employees from the Expectancy Theory perspective.

4. Equity Theory explains why employees can be happy and motivated with their work situation one day and with same work condition, can get demotivated if they learn that a colleague is enjoying a better reward–to–effort ratio. Hence, as much as possible the organization should strive hard to give a sense of fairness to all employees when it comes to reward–to–effort ratio.

5. From the Two Factor Theory of Herzberg, it can be understood that employee motivation factors are not extrinsic factors, but is very much connected with the satisfaction derived from the job itself. Hence, to motivate an employee, the job itself should be challenging and interesting and there should be scope for job enrichment. From this theory, the importance of job design, job enrichment, job enlargement, job rotation etc can be understood.

6. Goal Setting Theory is used in the workplace to improve and sustain performance of employees. Goal Setting Theory is based on the assumption that employees' behavior reflects their inner goals and motives. Some of the

ways that managers use this theory are:

- Include the employees in goal setting
- Set individual goals along with organizational goals
- Attach rewards along with the attainment of goals
- Provide continuous coaching and feedback

A popular application of Goal Setting Theory is MBO (Management by Objective).

MANAGEMENT BY OBJECTIVE

Management By Objective is a technique where employees and their managers sit together to set, record and monitor the goals for a specific period of time. The goals and planning in the organization flow from top to down involving all the members where organizational goals are transformed to personal goals. MBO involves continuous and ongoing tracking and feedback process. The term was pioneered by the Father of Modern Corporate Management, Peter Drucker in the 1960s in his book "The practice of management." MBO integrates the various hierarchical levels in the organization.

Some of MBO principles as per Peter Drucker are:

- Cascading of organizational goals and objectives
- Specific objectives for each member
- Participative decision-making
- Explicit time period
- Performance evaluation and feedback.

MBO goals are expected to be:

- Specific
- Measurable
- Attainable
- Realistic
- Time bound

Features of MBO

a) MBO is an attempt made to integrate the organizational and personal goals which lead to effective management

b) It combines long range and short range goals

c) MBO also relates societal goals with that of organizational goals.

d) It emphasizes effective performance along with the goals

e) It promotes an atmosphere of trust, honesty, and commitment.

Advantages of MBO

- It encourages detailed planning by managers who integrate the organizational goals with personal goals.
- Both the subordinates and supervisor are sure of what is expected out of them and hence have clarity about their work.
- It promotes proactive behavior and disciplined way of achieving the goals.
- MBO identifies the area or fields in which the employees need further training which would lead to career development.

- Effective communication occurs between the employees and supervisors which clear any ambiguity and confusion.
- Greater participation improves the morale of the employees as they feel a part of the decision-making the process of the organization.

Disadvantages of MBO

- It is a slow and time-consuming process
- It can succeed only if there is complete support from the top management
- It is quite complex to create comparative ratings of individuals as each of their goals differ form on another.
- It requires constant monitoring and revision which might become a distraction and shadow other important events to be undertaken.
- Some employees don't want the responsibility and goals. Such employees would practice some unethical behavior to eliminate their duties.

9 798885 461207

Printed by Libri Plureos GmbH in Hamburg, Germany